THE LORD OF THE RINGS

THE RETURN OF THE KING

PHOTO GUIDE

"We shall find it! Yes! We shall find the Precious and keep it for ourselves!"

First published in Great Britain by Collins in 2003
Collins is an imprint of HarperCollins*Publishers*, 77-85 Fulham Palace Road, Hammersmith, London W6 8JB

www.tolkien.co.uk

Text by David Brawn
Adapted from the screenplay by Fran Walsh, Philippa Boyens, Peter Jackson and Stephen Sinclair
Design by James Stevens, Production by Chris Wright

Photography by Pierre Vinet and Chris Coad

A catalogue record for this book is available from the British Library.

ISBN 0 00 717056 4

Printed and bound in Scotland by Scotprint

THE LORD OF THE RINGS
THE RETURN OF THE KING
PHOTO GUIDE

Collins
An imprint of HarperCollins*Publishers*

Sauron's plans for the conquest of Middle-earth are nearing completion. He is drawing together an army from regions throughout the land, including the fearsome Haradrim, Easterlings, Orcs and Trolls.

His nine Ringwraiths patrol the skies on wicked Fell Beasts, and his anger is growing. For the most unlikely of heroes are struggling to prevent Sauron's domination:

The Ents, ancient and normally peaceful tree-folk, have destroyed the fortress of his great ally, Saruman;

The rural-dwelling Riders of Rohan have defeated an army of specially bred Uruk-hai warriors at Helm's Deep;

And Gollum, a twisted halfling sent by Sauron to retrieve the One Ring, has disappeared from sight.

The ancient wizard Gandalf, thought killed in the Mines of Moria, is conspiring with the heir of Elendil to unite all the Free Peoples against the Dark Lord.

"If the Ring is destroyed, then Sauron will fall, and his fall will be so low that none will see his arising ever again. But if Sauron regains the Ring, his victory will be swift and complete."

As his daughter Arwen lies dying, Lord Elrond of the Elves arranges for the ancient shards of Narsil, the blade that cut down Sauron centuries ago, to be reforged into a new and mighty sword, a weapon so powerful that even the Dead begin to stir…

Pippin Took cannot sleep. The destruction of Isengard is playing on his mind, and he has become fascinated by Saruman's seeing stone, brought back by Gandalf from the Tower of Orthanc.

"What are you doing?"

"I just wanted to look at it…"

"Pippin – no!"

Aragorn snatches the palantír away. But it is too late – Gandalf realises the hobbit is now in great danger.

"Things are now in motion that cannot be undone. Sauron has looked into the face of young Peregrin Took and mistaken him for the Ring-bearer."

Gandalf decides he must take Pippin to safety. As they ride out on Shadowfax, Pippin's friend Merry asks where they are going.

"To the safest place in Middle-earth... the city of Minas Tirith."

Frodo Baggins, weighed down by the burden of carrying the One Ring to Mordor, now has two companions to encourage him: his faithful servant Sam Gamgee, and their new guide Gollum.

"Come on, we must go, no time, no time to lose."

They reach a crossroads where the ancient statue of a Gondorian king sits, still and solemn. Orcs have toppled the statue's head and replaced it with a crude carving. Frodo is saddened by it.

"These lands were once part of the Kingdom of Gondor… long ago when there was a king and the West stood strong."

As they continue on, Sam overhears Gollum talking to himself.

"Let her deal with them. She must eat… the Precious will be ours once the hobbitses are dead!"

"Minas Tirith!
The greatest stronghold
of Middle-earth."

Entering the White City, Gandalf and Pippin ride up hundreds of steps to the seventh level, the Court of the Kings, a thousand feet above the ground.

"Gandalf, why are they guarding a dead tree?"

Gandalf explains how the White Tree has withered as the rule of Gondor has waned. The citadel guards protect the tree in the belief that it, like Gondor, might one day flourish once more.

In the throne room, Gandalf meets Denethor, the Ruling Steward of Gondor. He is a gloomy and bitter old man, who is angry about the death of his son Boromir, and he warns Gandalf that Aragorn will not be welcome here.

"The rule of Gondor is mine, and no other's!"

"Authority is not given to you, Steward Gondor, to deny the return of the King."

When Gandalf has gone, Denethor is reunited with his second son, Faramir. He is furious that Faramir has allowed Frodo to take the Ring of Power into Mordor when he could have brought it back here. He reminds himself of the two brothers before they left.

"Boromir would have remembered his father's need. He would have brought me a kingly gift!"

Pippin is on a mission for Gandalf. Creeping on to the battlements, he lights the massive beacon on top of the city. It is a signal to others that war has begun.

Across the plains at Edoras, Aragorn bursts into the Golden Hall.

"The beacons of Minas Tirith! Gondor calls for aid!"

As King Théoden rallies the Riders of Rohan, he receives an unexpected offer.

*"I have a sword.
I offer you my service,
Théoden King."*

*"Gladly I receive it –
you shall be Meriadoc,
Esquire of Rohan,
and ride with me."*

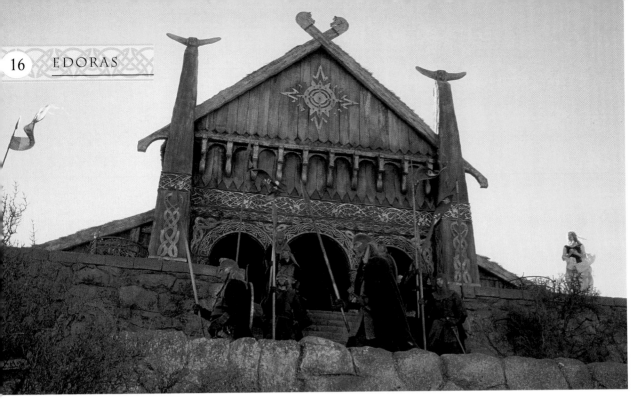

As the Rohirrim ride out, the lady Éowyn watches them go. She decides to follow them…

Pippin has joined the Tower Guard. He has been given the only hobbit-sized uniform they have – it was made for Faramir when he was just a boy.

Meanwhile, Faramir leads 200 knights out of the city to go and confront the evil forces that have invaded the neighbouring city of Osgiliath.

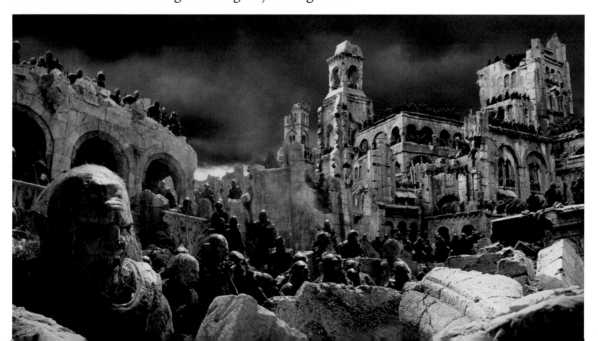

Night has fallen and the Riders of Rohan have set up camp at Dunharrow. Aragorn is summoned to meet an unexpected guest in King Théoden's tent. He has a gift for Aragorn.

"Andúril, flame of the West … forged from the shards of Narsil. The man who can wield the power of this sword can summon to him an army more deadly than any that walk this earth!"

Aragorn realises what he must do – go to summon the Oath-breakers who dwell in the haunted mountain, from where none have ever returned.

"Every path you have trod, through wilderness, through war, has led to this road. This is your test, Aragorn."

Gimli and Legolas insist on accompanying their friend on his new quest.

"We're going to follow you, lad – even on the dark Road…"
"…To wherever it may lead."

The next day, the entire camp is on the move – they ride to war. Merry is preparing to go with them, but King Théoden has other ideas.

"Little hobbits do not belong in war, Master Meriadoc."

"I want to fight!"

Then, as all hope seems lost, a young rider pulls Merry up on to a horse.

Faramir's horse has returned to Minas Tirith, dragging its badly wounded master behind it. His men were ambushed by the Orcs at Osgiliath.

"They were outnumbered, none survived."

Denethor is heartbroken – he believes both his sons are now dead.

"The House of Stewards has failed! My line has ended."

"The living are not welcome on this road."

Aragorn, Legolas and Gimli make their way up a gloomy canyon to the Dwimorberg Mountain. It is a desolate and eerie place.

"Long ago the men of the mountain swore an oath to the last King ofGondor to come to his aid... Isildur cursed them never to rest until they fulfilled their pledge."

"Who enters my domain?"

In the dark passages under the mountain, ghoulish hands reach up out of the mist, and a mummified spectre looms out of the fog ahead of them. It is the King of the Dead.

"None but the King of Gondor may command me!"

Raising his sacred sword in answer, Aragorn addresses the ghost army.

"Fight and regain your honour. Fight and I will release you from this living death!"

Minas Tirith is under attack. The vast Orc army has advanced from Osgiliath, and great siege towers and mighty wooden catapults now surround the city. With the lower level already in flames, the huge gate is smashed open.

Arriving outside the city, King Théoden orders his men to join the battle.

"Fear no darkness! Ride now, ride to ruin and the world's ending!"

On the battlements, the soldiers of Gondor watch in awe as the charge of the Rohirrim closes in on the Orc army.

High above the fighting, Denethor leads a procession carrying Faramir's unconscious body. He has planned a noble death for him and his son.

"No tomb for Denethor and Faramir... we will burn like the heathen kings of old!"

Pippin realises in horror that the Steward of Gondor is quite mad!

"Denethor has lost his mind. He's burning Faramir alive!"

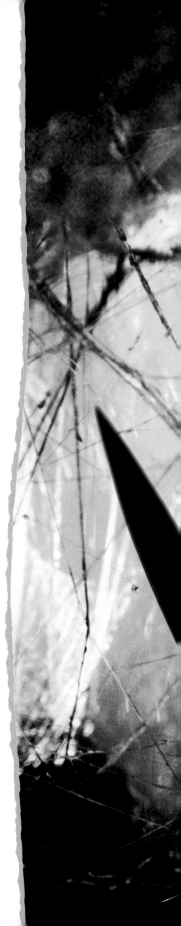

Frodo advances into the pass of Cirith Ungol, a dark tunnel through the mountains. It is filled with rotting things and the odour of unspeakable decay, and as they move forward, Frodo hears a gurgling, venomous hiss from the shadows.

"What was that? Sméagol?"

But Gollum has deserted him!

In the darkness, Frodo remembers Galadriel's gift − the star-glass of Eärendil. He pulls it from his jacket, but the light it casts reveals a nightmare... Shelob, a huge and loathsome Spider!

Shagrat and Gorbag – an
Uruk and an Orc – come to
Shelob's lair to scavenge for
her spoils. They find Frodo's
lifeless body.

*"Looks like old Shelob's
been having some fun!"*

*"The little filth'll
wake up in a
few hours..."*

*"...And then he'll wish
he'd never
been born!"*

In the dark Orc watch-tower at Cirith Ungol, Frodo wakes to find himself a prisoner. He freezes, as Gorbag climbs into the room.

"I'm gonna bleed you like a stuck pig!"

Just then, a rescuer appears out of the shadows.

"Sam!!!"

Disguising themselves as Orcs, Frodo and Sam leave the tower and set out for Mount Doom. They have entered Sauron's realm of Mordor, and are at last within sight of their goal!

The spectral warriors of the Army of the Dead swarm over Minas Tirith, finishing off the remaining invaders. With their oath fulfilled, Aragorn releases the King of the Dead from their bond, to be at peace.

The battlefield has fallen silent. Sauron's army has been defeated, but it is a scene of devastation, where the bodies outnumber the living.

Pippin is relieved to find Merry is only wounded.

"Come on Merry, up you get, we must get you to the city…"

At Minas Tirith, Faramir lies dying. Helping the elderly nurse Ioreth, Aragorn administers an ancient remedy to his fallen comrade.

"It is said in old lore that the hands of a king are the hands of a healer..."

"I'll be an Orc no more, and I will bear no weapon, fair or foul."

Reaching Mount Doom, Frodo and Sam discard their Orc clothing and struggle against the heat and ash as they approach the Crack of Doom. Frodo is exhausted, and Sam offers him the last of their water.

"There will be none left for the return journey."

"I don't think there will be a return journey, Mr Frodo."

Arwen is gravely ill. She senses that Sauron is about to regain the Ring, and that the world of Men is almost at an end. With Sauron's death all that will save her, she tells Elrond of her love for Aragorn.

"I wish I could have seen him one last time."

Knowing that Frodo must be near his goal, and therefore in great danger, Aragorn decides to lead a force of Men to the Black Gates of Mordor. He hopes to distract Sauron and his remaining forces long enough for Frodo to destroy the Ring and break Sauron's power forever.

Riding out, Aragorn, clad in the armour of his forebears, knows he carries the hopes for the future of Middle-earth with him.

Sam and Frodo reach the stone doorway of Sammath Naur, the way into the mountain where the Ring was made. As they stagger inside, the fierce heat is overwhelming.

They do not notice the presence of a familiar figure who has been waiting for them…

*"My Precious!
My Preciousss!"*

Suddenly Gollum appears and tries to claim the Ring for himself. But he is too late!

"And thus it was that a Fourth Age of Middle-earth began, and the Fellowship of the Ring, though eternally bound by friendship and love, was ended."